IGUANA IN THE ROAD

By Lori Bonati

Illustrated by Diane Ronning

Iguana in the Road

Written by Lori Bonati
Illustrated by Diane Ronning

Text © 2023 by Lori Bonati
Illustrations © 2023 by Diane Ronning

All rights reserved.

No part of this publication may be reproduced or transmitted in any form or by any means without prior written permission of the publisher or copyright holder except for the use of brief quotations in a book review.

ISBN: 9798389142787
Juvenile Nonfiction > Animals > Reptiles & Amphibians
Juvenile Nonfiction > Animals > Animal Welfare

Published by Lyric Power Publishing LLC, Tucson, AZ.

Dedicated to

Elaine and Susan

IGUANA IN THE ROAD

By Lori Bonati

Illustrated by Diane Ronning

I am an iguana.
I live on an island road.
I am *not* …

a crocodile, a turtle, or a toad.

All iguanas are lizards,
but we're not all the same.
There are many iguana species,

Fiji Banded

Spiny Tail

Cayman Blue

Green

Rhinoceros

Rock Iguana is MY name.

Iguanas are quite beautiful.
We have such lovely scales,
and something else we're proud of is …

our

very

lengthy

tails!

But often, we have trouble
when across our roads we roam,
and so we are endangered here
upon our island home.

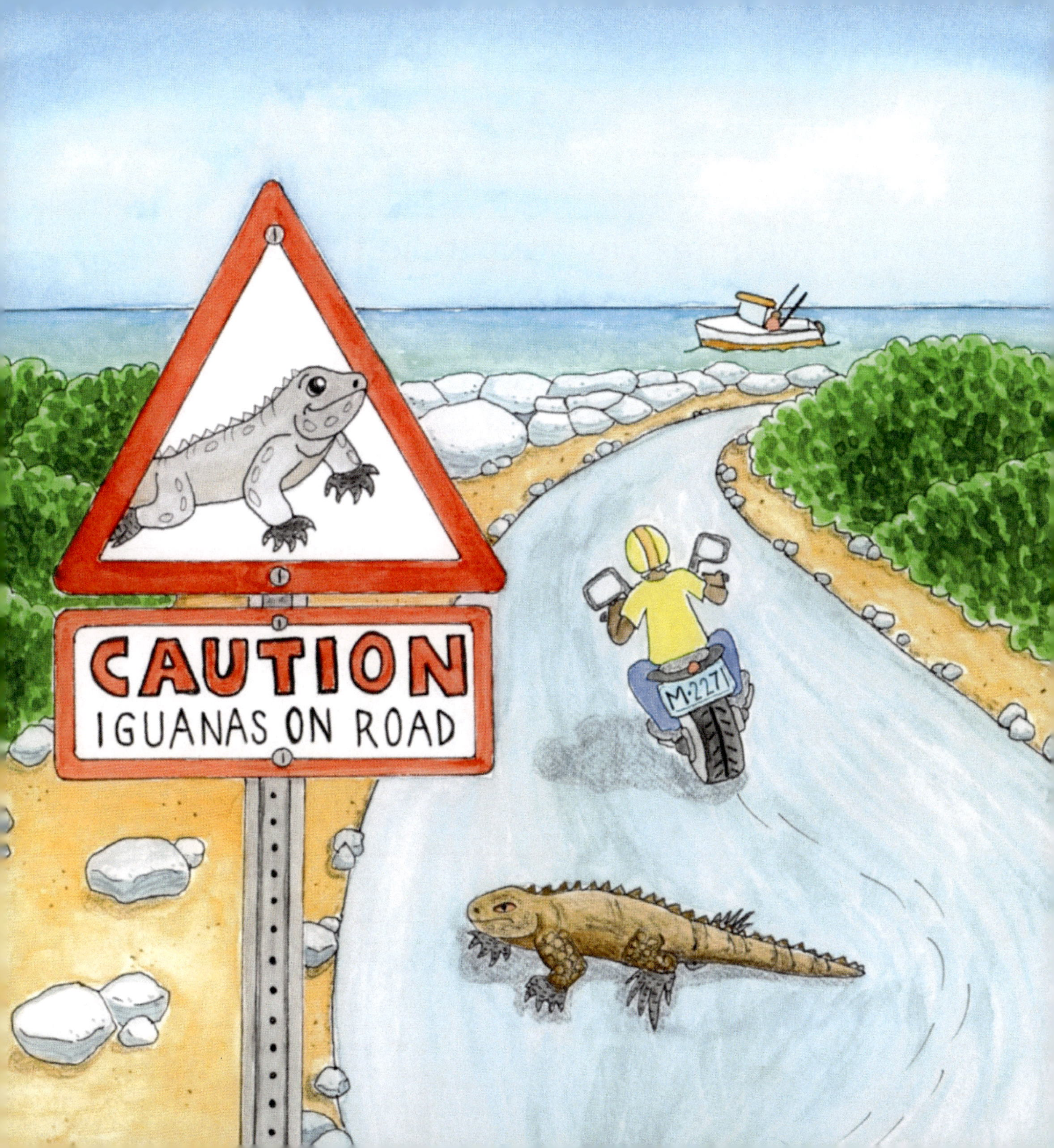
CAUTION
IGUANAS ON ROAD
M·2271

Sometimes we want to lie there
soaking up a little heat,
because we're ectotherms, you see.
We get warmth from the street.

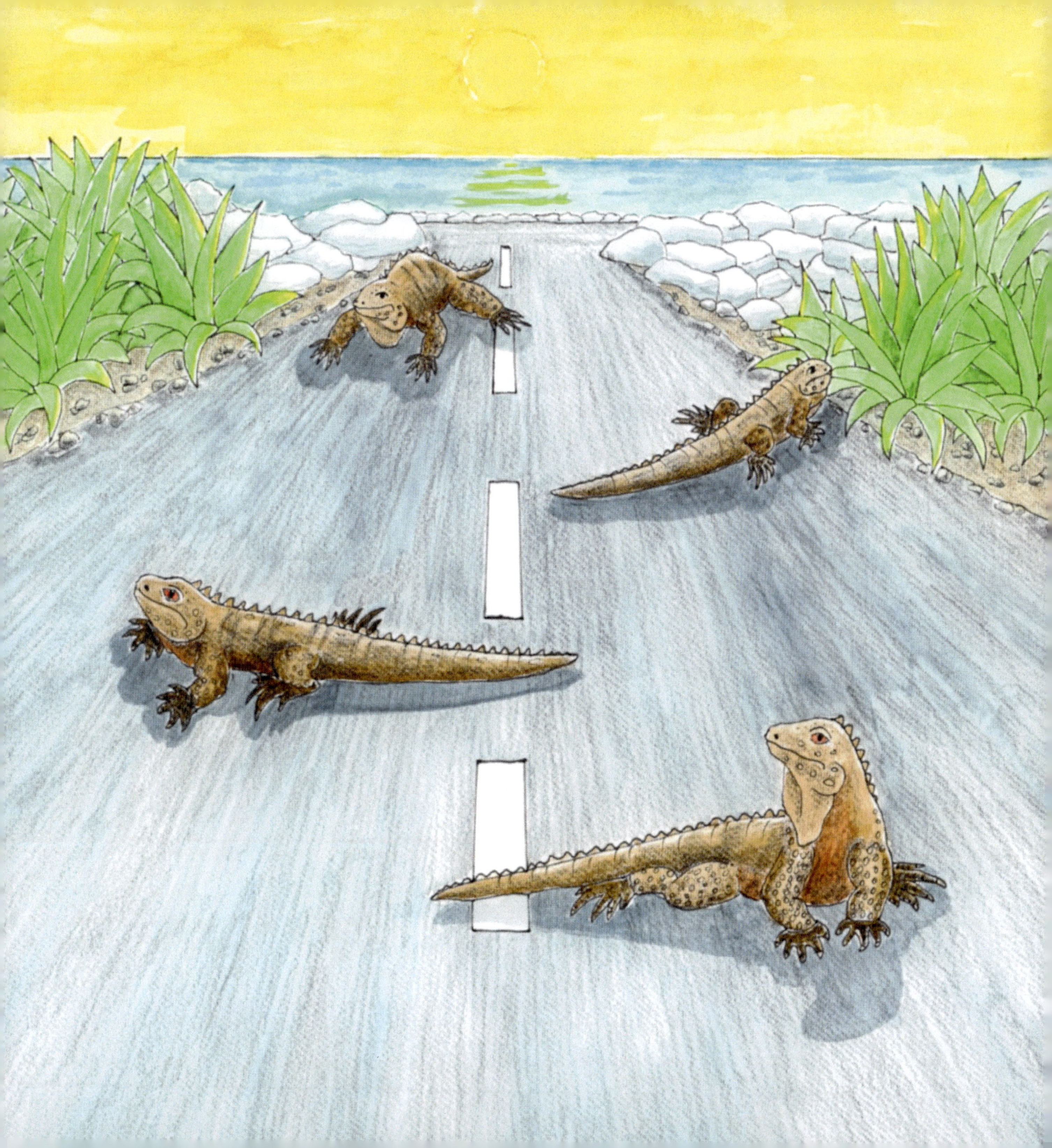

But roadways have so many cars!
They can be really busy.
When I see traffic moving fast,
it makes me kind of dizzy.

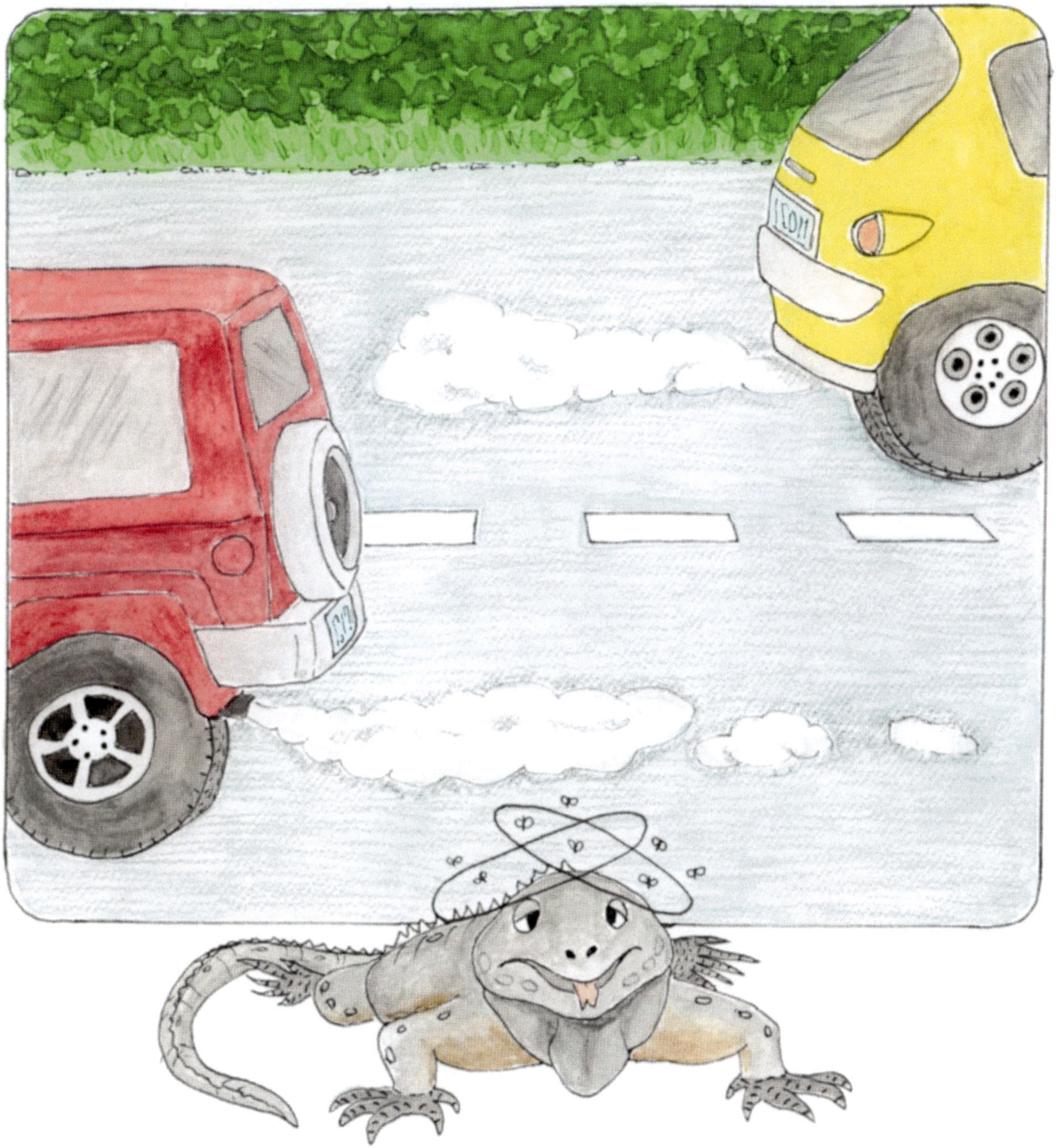

And something else I've noticed
and I thought that I should mention -
too many people text and drive!
They do not pay attention!

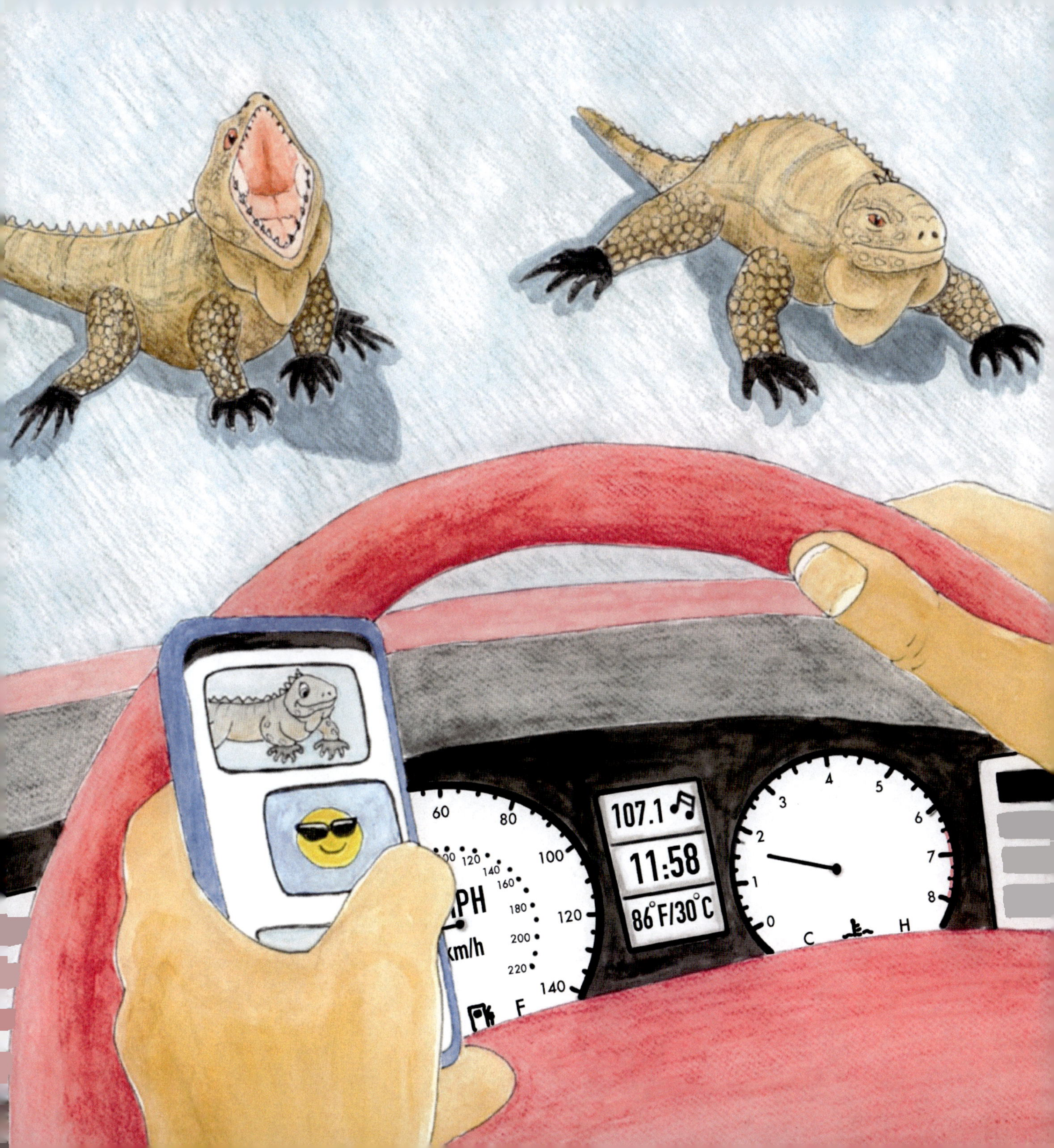

107.1
11:58
86°F/30°C
60
80
100
120
140
PH
km/h
C
H
F

Iguanas know how to escape
from snakes and birds of prey,
but cars are something new to us,
and we get in their way.

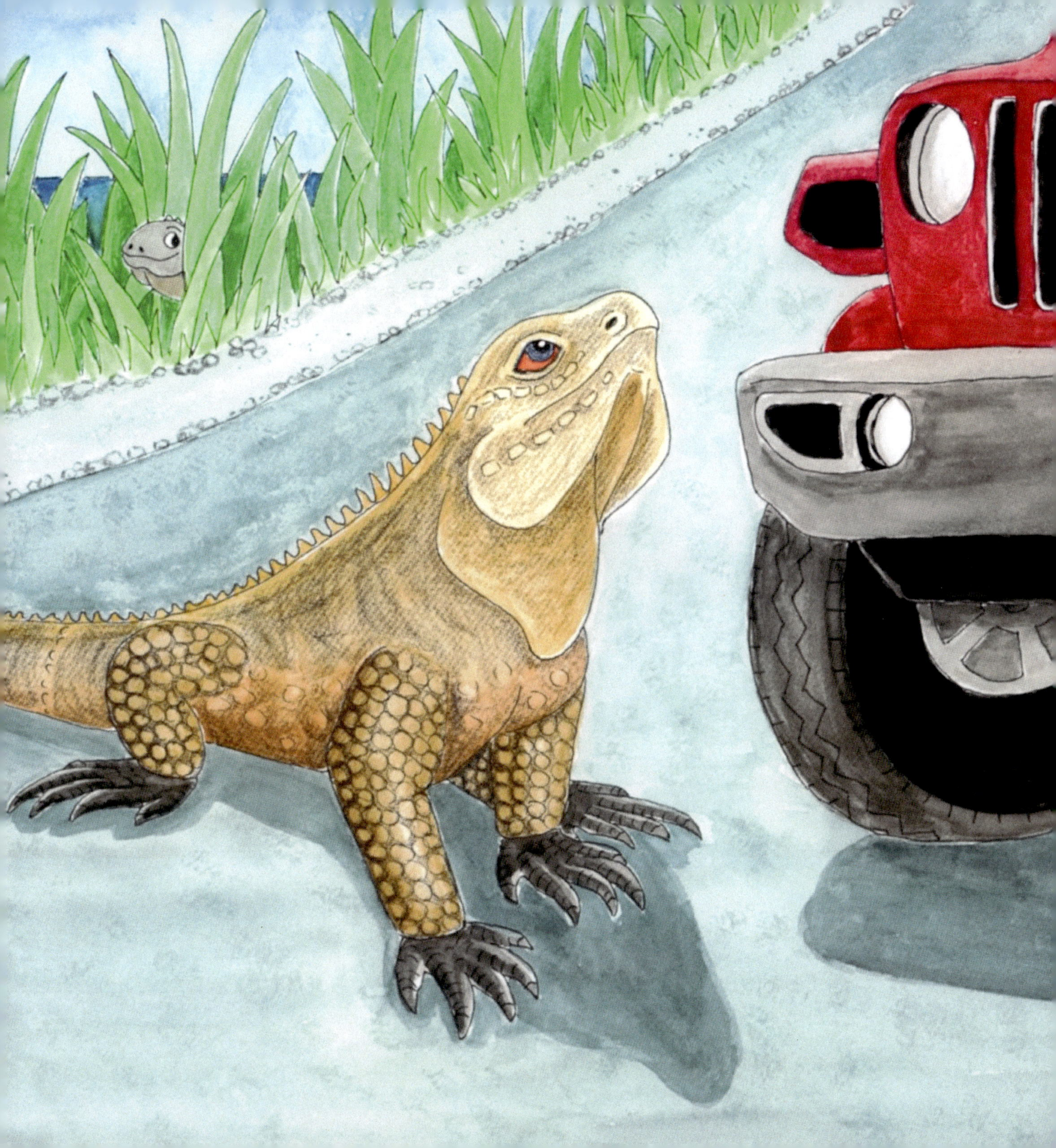

So, if you are out driving,
can you go a little slower?
We like it when you take your time,

IGUANAS!
DRIVE SLOWLY

so you won't run us over.

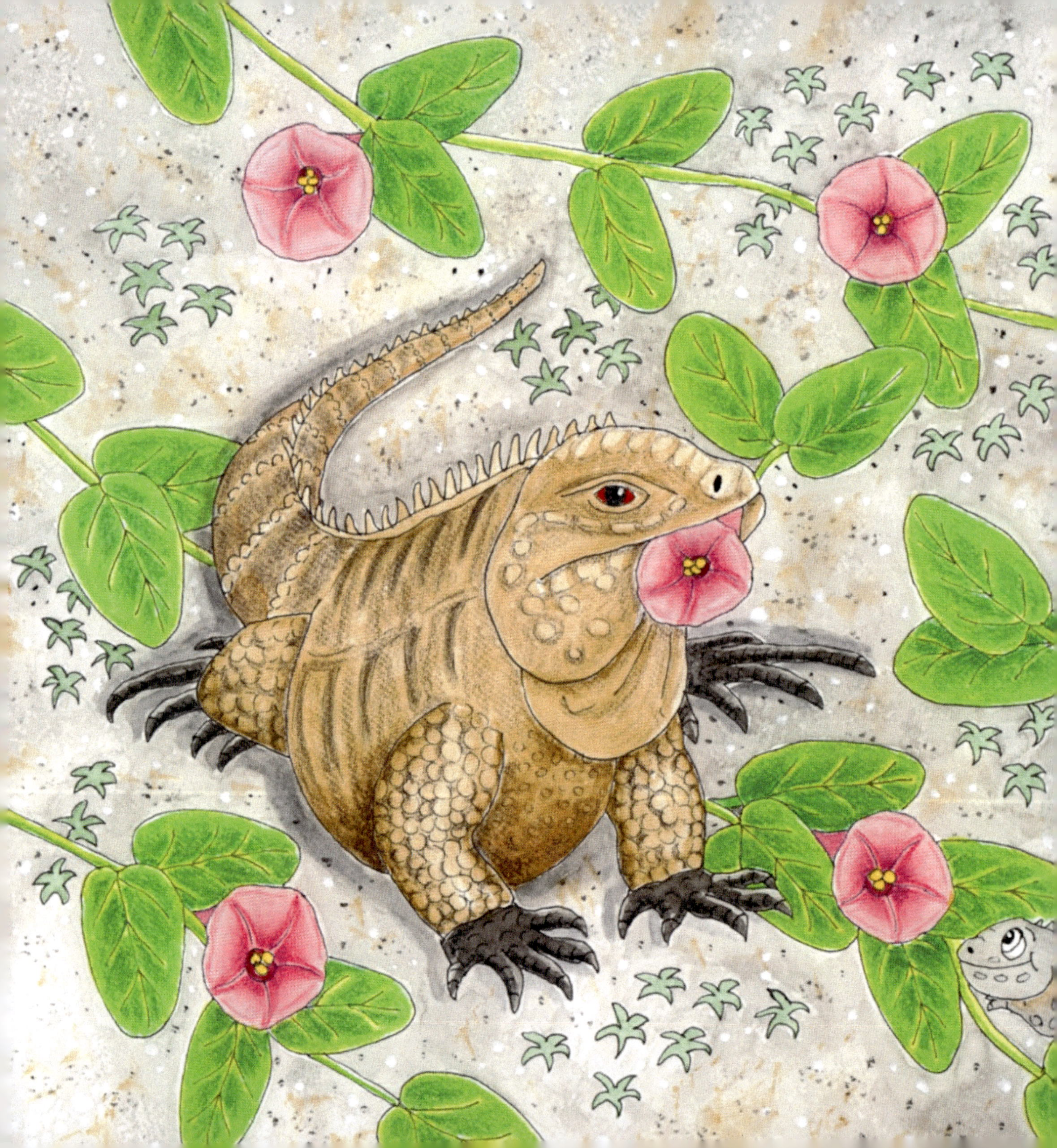

Iguanas are important,
since we help plants grow and thrive
by eating and dispersing seeds.
Please help us stay alive!

Why, thank you, friend, for waiting
while across this road I scurry.
You've made it safe for me to cross …

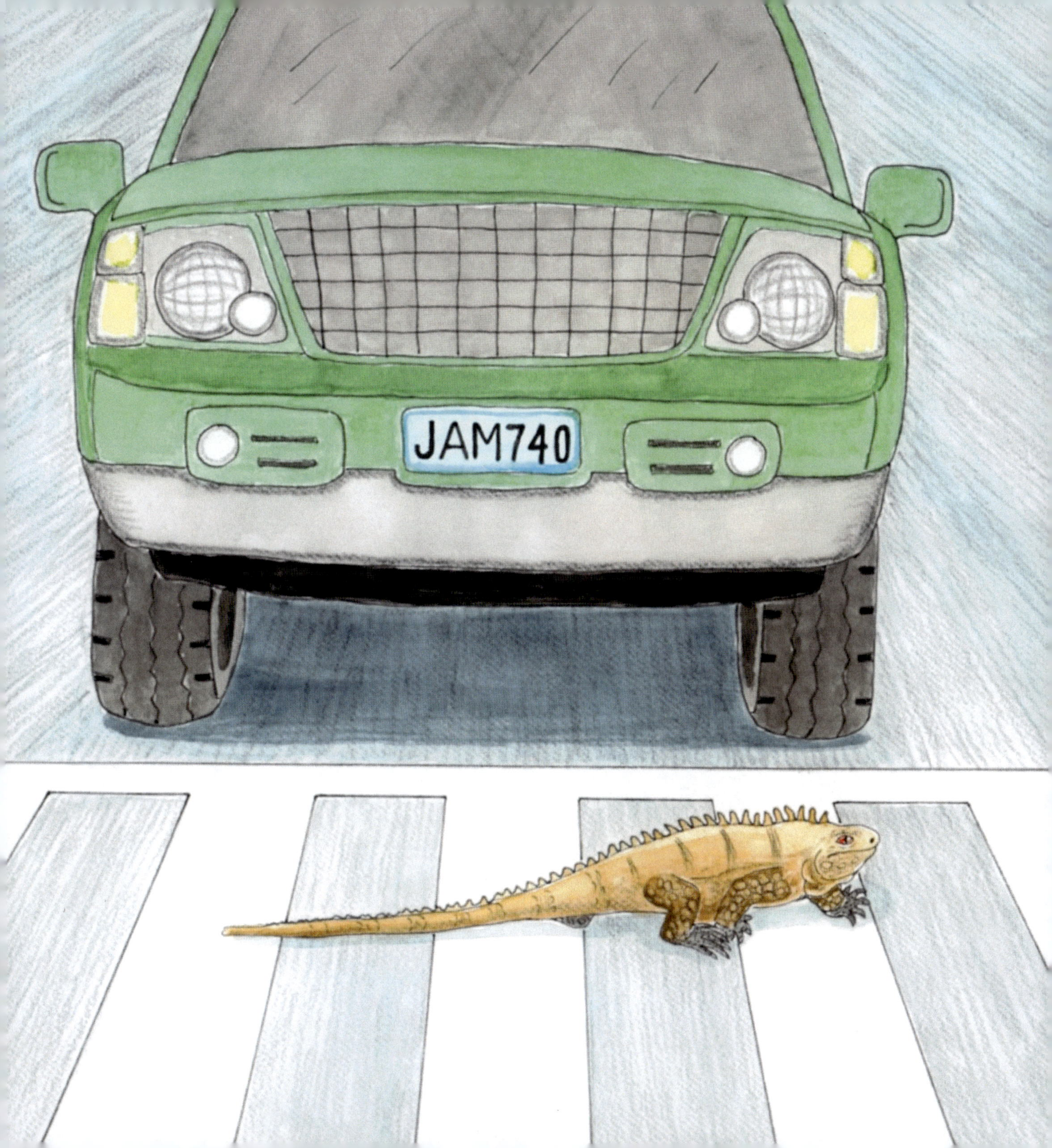
JAM740

now I don't have to worry!

FASCINATING IGUANA FACTS

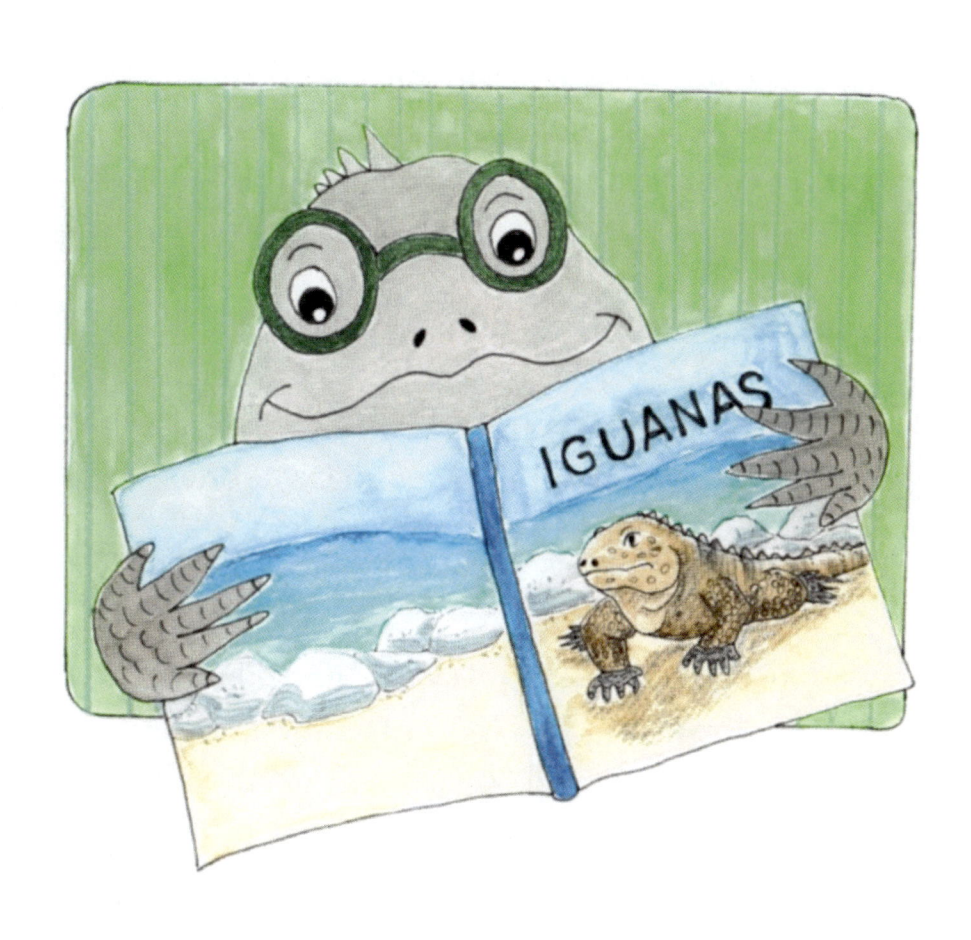

Fascinating Iguana Facts

What kind of animal is an iguana?
An iguana is a lizard, a type of reptile in the animal kingdom. Its family is *Iguanidae*. Within this family, there are nine branches. Each of these branches is called a genus.

How long have iguana-like lizards existed?
The oldest known iguanian fossil, *Magnuviator ovimonsensis*, is 75 million years old. It was discovered in a dinosaur nesting site in Montana, USA.

How many different species of iguanas are there?
There are many different types of iguanas (spiny tail, Galapagos, green, desert, marine, etc.). Within the genus *Cyclura*, also known as "rock iguanas," there currently are believed to be ten species and five subspecies.

Where do iguanas live?
Iguanas are found only in the Western Hemisphere (North America, Central America, and South America) and on the Fiji Islands. Rock iguanas are native to the Caribbean islands, where they live in dry forest areas.

Tell me more about rock iguanas.
Rock iguanas are a relatively new genus, having been in existence for only 15 to 35 million years. They are known for their high degree of "endemism," meaning that only one, or very few, species of rock iguanas live on each island or group of islands. Rock iguana species include: Anegada ground iguana, Cuban iguana, Grand Cayman blue iguana, Jamaican iguana, Mona Island iguana, Northern Bahamian rock iguana, Rhinoceros iguana, Ricord's iguana, San Salvador iguana, and Turks and Caicos rock iguana. The story in this book is about a subspecies of the Cuban iguana known as the Sister Islands rock iguana, or *Cyclura nubila caymanensis*.

Are iguanas hot-blooded or cold-blooded?
Iguanas, like all other reptiles, are cold-blooded. (Another name for cold-blooded is "ectotherm.") Cold-blooded does not mean that they have cold blood. It just means that their entire body temperature depends on the temperature of the environment. An ectotherm can regulate its temperature by basking in the sun or by moving into its den or to another shady spot.

What kind of climate do iguanas prefer?
Iguanas live in warm climates. Rock iguanas live in the arid regions of the Caribbean islands, where the limestone earth has been eroded and has formed karst (worn away soft rock that may contain caves and sinkholes).

What do iguanas eat?
Iguanas are folivores (which means that they eat the leaves and flowers of plants), but they also are known as "opportunistic" feeders. They will eat animal protein if they happen to come across it.

How long do iguanas live?
Adult iguanas can live a long time in their natural environments. Although rock iguanas can live 50 years, most are now considered to be critically endangered (in danger of becoming extinct).

Why are rock iguanas endangered?
Unfortunately, people are responsible for the declining numbers of rock iguanas. They have destroyed iguana habitats by building roads and houses where iguanas live, and they have introduced invasive green iguanas and animals that attack iguanas (raccoons, rats, and pets like cats and dogs). Motorists who drive carelessly are a significant cause of death for rock iguanas, striking and killing them on island roads.

How do rock iguanas help plants to survive?
Rock iguanas help plants in the Caribbean to survive by eating them! After they are eaten, the plants' seeds travel through the iguanas' digestive systems and are dispersed (spread), rather than remaining in one location where they would have to compete with each other for water, light, and soil nutrients. Throughout the Caribbean, there are about 11,000 different species of plants that germinate (grow) from

seeds, and many of these are facing the possibility of extinction. Rock iguanas can help prevent plant extinction.

Does anything eat rock iguanas?
Adult rock iguanas have very few natural predators, but young hatchlings and juveniles are prey for birds and snakes. Domesticated dogs and cats will kill rock iguanas of any age. Adult rock iguanas who have never been chased or attacked by these animals have grown up without fear of them. Sometimes people use rock iguanas as food, too.

How do iguanas defend themselves?
An iguana's first line of defense is flight. They can run very fast, so they are able to successfully flee from predators. If an attacker gets too close, though, the iguana will whip its tail at the predator. Finally, if all else fails, the iguana will bite its attacker.

What happens if an iguana loses its tail in a fight?
In the event of a predator attack, an iguana can "drop" its tail (let the predator have it). The detached tail will wiggle for a while after it's been dropped, distracting the predator and allowing the iguana to make a quick getaway. The iguana will live to tell the "tail," and a young iguana's tail will even grow back! This is called "autotomy." However, the iguana's new tail is never as pretty as the original one.

Why are iguanas' tails so long?
Iguanas use their tails for balance and to store fat.

What is an iguana's skin made of?
Iguanas, like most reptiles, have scales and are not at all slimy! Iguana scales are made of keratin, a protein that makes up our hair, skin, and nails. An iguana's keratin scales form a dry, hard layer around its body, giving it armor-like protection and preventing water loss.

How big do iguanas get?
Iguanas come in all sizes, from about 1 to 5 feet (.3 to 1.5 meters) in total length.

Are iguanas kept in zoos?
Yes. Not only do zoos care for iguanas, but they are active in conservation efforts, too. One example is the San Diego Zoo in California (USA), which has an active rock iguana conservation program, including breeding and educational outreach. Another center that promotes reptile research and conservation is IguanaLand, in Punta Gorda, Florida (USA).

Can I keep an iguana as a pet?
Rock iguanas are not usually kept as pets. (Green iguanas are the ones people tend to have as pets.) Certain non-endangered, captive-

bred iguana species can be kept as pets, but they have specific and complicated care needs, including temperature, humidity, food, and size of enclosure.

Do iguanas have personalities?
Yes, iguanas have personalities, temperaments, and emotions. Some are more docile than others. Their body language tells you whether they are feeling relaxed or stressed. In captivity, they can be socialized, and they will recognize their owners.

Do iguanas get along with other pets?
Iguanas can coexist peacefully with other animals under the right conditions. An iguana will probably be bothered or frightened by a cat or a dog. Fights between iguanas and these pets can happen, so it's important to separate them in your home, and to supervise all animal "meetings." An iguana's temperament can change during mating season, so keep an extra-careful eye on your iguana during that time.

How can I help iguanas?
You can help protect rock iguanas by learning all you can about them, talking to others about them, and driving safely (or encouraging others to do so). You can also become involved in iguana conservation efforts in your area. Here are some websites to get you started:

- International Iguana Foundation: IguanaFoundation.org
- International Reptile Conservation Foundation: IRCF.org
- International Union for Conservation of Nature (IUCN), Iguana Specialist Group: IUCN-ISG.org

How can I learn more about iguanas?

For more information (and even a song) about iguanas, go to:

- Website: ElaineAPowers.com
- Iguana Song: https://www.youtube.com/watch?v=7J1MzU-Fcy4
- YouTube: @elainepowers9234
- Lyric Power Publishing: LyricPower.net

About the Author:

Lori Bonati lives in upstate New York. Following a career as a school psychologist, she embraced writing and now creates stories and poems for children and adults. Her other passions include photography, songwriting, hiking, baking, and travel. She loves spending time with family, friends, and her dog, Maya. You can contact her through her website, LoriBonati.com.

Other books by Lori Bonati:

- **Wordle Poems: A Poem a Day for Wordle Nerds (Books 1, 2, and 3)**
- **Standing in the Surf**

About the Illustrator:

Diane Ronning lives in southern Arizona where she paints and photographs wildlife. After a long career teaching art, she began illustrating children's books. She and her husband like to visit their four grandchildren, two little grand-dogs, and rescue cat. She hopes this book will save many iguanas.

Other books illustrated by Diane Ronning:

- ***How to Eat Breakfast,*** by Gene Twaronite

Acknowledgments

Many thanks to my illustrator, Diane Ronning, for her expert collaboration on this project. In addition, I am grateful to Elaine A. Powers and to Susan Oyler, dedicated members of my writing critique group, for their inspiration, constructive comments, and support.

©2023 All Rights Reserved.

Made in the USA
Middletown, DE
15 September 2024